A Guide to French Grammar

Third Edition

Stanley Prince

*Drawings by
Richard Walker*

PACKARD PUBLISHING LIMITED
CHICHESTER

A Guide to French Grammar
Third edition

© Stanley R. Prince 1975, 1992, 1994, 2014

This revised edition published in 2014 by Packard Publishing Limited,
14 Guilden Road, Chichester, West Sussex, PO19 7LA, UK.

All rights reserved. No part of this publication may be reproduced, stored in a retrieval system or transmitted in any form or by any means, electronic, mechanical, photocopying, recording or otherwise, without the prior permission of the publisher.

ISBN 978 185341 141 0

A CIP cataloguing record of this book is available from the British Library.

Cover photograph of Mont St Michel, Normandy.

Prepared for press by Michael Packard.
Layout by Hilite Design & Reprographics Limited,
Marchwood, Southampton, Hampshire.
Printed and bound by PublishPoint, KnowledgePoint Limited,
Winnersh, Wokingham, Berkshire.

CONTENTS

PART A *GRAMMAR*

1	VERBS	1
1.1	Present Tense	1
1.2	Perfect Tense	9
1.3	Pluperfect Tense	12
1.4	Imperfect Tense	12
1.5	Future Tense	13
1.6	Conditional Tense	14
1.7	Imperative Mood (command form)	15
1.8	Infinitives	16
1.9	Present Participles	16
1.10	Verbs followed by à	17
1.11	Verbs followed by de	18
1.12	Entrer dans	19
1.13	Verbs which include the English Preposition	19
1.14	The Passive Voice	19
2	NOUNS	21
2.1	Gender of Nouns	21
2.2	Plurals of Nouns	22
3	PRONOUNS	23
3.1	Personal Pronouns	23
3.2	Interrogative Pronouns	25
3.3	Demonstrative Pronouns	26
3.4	Relative Pronouns	26
3.5	Possessive Pronouns	27
4	ADJECTIVES	28
4.1	Agreement of Adjectives with Noun	28
4.2	Position of Adjectives	30
4.3	Interrogative Adjectives	30
4.4	Demonstrative Adjectives	30
4.5	Possessive Adjectives	31
5	ADVERBS	31
5.1	Formation	31
5.2	Common Irregular Adverbs	31
6	PREPOSITIONS	32
6.1	Some Important Prepositions	32
6.2	Countries	33
6.3	Continents	33
6.4	Prepositional Phrases	34
7	NEGATIVES	35
8	USES OF *DE*	36

	9	IDIOMS	36
	9.1	with *Avoir*	36
	9.2	with *Faire*	37
	9.3	*Venir de*	37
	9.4	Tenses with *depuis*	37
	9.5	*Être en train de*	38
	9.6	C'est; il est	38
PART B	**MISCELLANEOUS INFORMATION**		**39**
	10.1	Distinguish between …	39
	10.2	*L'Alphabet Français*	39
	10.3	Accents	40
	10.4	Days - *Les Jours de La Semaine*	40
	10.5	Months - *Les Mois de L'Année*	41
	10.6	Seasons	41
	10.7	Numbers	42
	10.8	Date	42
	10.9	Time	43
	10.10	Linguistic Subtleties	43
PART C	**COMPREHENSION**		**45**
	11.1	Question Words	45
	11.2	Important Questions	45
PART D	**PRONUNCIATION**		**47**
	12.1	Sounds	47
	12.2	Homonyms	49
PART E	**FAUX-AMIS**		**51**
PART F	ESSAY WRITING		57
PART G	**JUST FOR FUN**		**58**
	15.1	Tongue Twisters	58
	15.2	Conundrum	58
	15.3	Quick Quiz	58
	15.4 Proverbs		59
PART H	**SUPPLEMENT**		**60**
	16.1	Past Historic Tense	60
	16.2	Past Anterior Tense	62
	16.3	Subjunctive Mood	63
	16.4	Formation of the Present Subjunctive	63
	16.5	Uses of the Subjunctive	65
	17	Answers to Quiz and Proverbs	66
	18	Glossary of Grammatical Terms	67

FOREWORD TO THE THIRD EDITION

This new edition has afforded me the opportunity, both to redraft the original text and add to its content. Sections covering verbs requiring à or *de,* and the passive voice, have been included for completeness, while the listing of prepositional phrases and *faux-amis* stems from an awareness of how such information has helped my own pupils to avoid linguistic pitfalls, as well as from my personal fascination with the vagaries of language, which I hope to share with my readers. The inclusion of cartoons, tongue twisters, a conundrum and a quiz are further innovations which should provide some welcome relief from the inevitably more serious process of learning.

The main aim, however, remains unchanged. It is to provide students with easy access to all the information required for revision at a glance, and I have endeavoured to produce a handy reference book of key facts and grammatical rules, as well as guides to the tackling of comprehension work and essay writing. The contents provide a full survey of traditional grammatical points, and should be an ideal way to consolidate, revise or check for gaps in one's knowledge. I do not take the slightest issue with the current emphasis on communication skills, but it is becoming increasingly recognized that language is not always best learned simply by a form of osmosis, and that some sort of mental application is probably required if real mastery is to be achieved. Thus, my book may well be viewed as a formal back-up to much of the 'softer' illustrative material currently on offer.

Finally, I should like to acknowledge the encouragement I have received from my publisher and former pupils. It is gratifying to learn that previous editions of my book were used by students not only at Common Entrance, GCE and GCSE levels but also at 'A' level and beyond. Good luck with this new edition and happy reading!

S.R.P., Hove, 2014

Part A
GRAMMAR

1 VERBS

1.1 Present Tense — *le présent*

Regular verbs:

Donner — to give

Je donne — give, I am giving
Tu donnes — You give, you are giving
Il donne — He gives, he is giving
Elle donne — She gives, she is giving
Nous donnons — We give, we are giving
Vous donnez — You give, you are giving
Ils donnent — They give, are giving (m)
Elles donnent — They give, are giving (f)

Finir — to finish		*Vendre* — to sell	
Je finis	— I finish, *etc.*	*Je vends*	— I sell, etc.
Tu finis	— You finish	*Tu vends*	— You sell
Il finit	— He finishes	*Il vend*	— He sells
Elle finit	— She finishes	*Elle vend*	— She sells
Nous finissons	— We finish	*Nous vendons*	— We sell
Vous finissez	— You finish	*Vous vendez*	— You sell
Ils finissent	— They finish (m)	*Ils vendent*	— They sell (m)
Elles finissent	— They finish (f)	*Elles vendent*	— They sell (f)

Four important irregular verbs:

Être	— to be	*Avoir*	— to have
Je suis	— I am	*J'ai*	— I have
Tu es	— You are	*Tu as*	— You have
Il est	— He is	*Il a*	— He has
Elle est	— She is	*Elle a*	— She has
Nous sommes	— We are	*Nous avons*	— We have
Vous êtes	— You are	*Vous avez*	— You have
Ils sont	— They are (m)	*Ils ont*	— They have (m)
Elles sont	— They are (f)	*Elles ont*	— They have (f)

Aller	— to go	**Faire**	— to do, to make
Je vais	— I go	*Je fais*	— I do
Tu vas	— You go	*Tu fais*	— You do
Il va	— He goes	*Il fait*	— He does
Elle va	— She goes	*Elle fait*	— She does
Nous allons	— We go	*Nous faisons*	— We do
Vous allez	— You go	*Vous faites*	— You do
Ils vont	— They go (m)	*Ils font*	— They do (m)
Elles vont	— They go (f)	*Elles font*	— They do (f)

NB. (1) These are the only four verbs which end in *-ont*. *All* others end in a silent *-ent* in 3rd person plural.
(2) Care! Vous *êtes*; Vous *faites*. *Also* Vous *dites*. All others end in *-ez* in 2nd person plural.

Irregular -ER verbs:

NB. (1) *Aller* is the only completely irregular verb;
(2) *Appeler* and *jeter* double the final consonant;
(3) *Acheter, lever, mener* take a grave accent in the singular; and
(4) *Espérer, sécher*, etc. — the acute accent changes to grave in the 3rd person plural;
(5) *Envoyer, essuyer, nettoyer* — y changes to an i;
(6) *Nous commençons; Nous mangeons.*

} in singular and 3rd person plural

Grammar: Irregular Verbs

Irregular *-IR* verbs:

Some -IR verbs go like:
Dormir — to sleep **Courir** — to run

Je dors *Je cours*
Tu dors *Tu cours*
Il dort *Il court*
Elle dort *Elle court*
Nous dormons *Nous courons*
Vous dormez *Vous courez*
Ils dorment *Ils courent*
Elles dorment *Elles courent*

e.g., *partir*, to leave; *sortir*, to go out; *mentir*, to (tell a) lie; *sentir*, to feel; *servir*, to serve.

Ouvrir — to open **Venir** — to come

J'ouvre *Je viens*
Tu ouvres *Tu viens*
Il ouvre *Il vient*
Elle ouvre *Elle vient*
Nous ouvrons *Nous venons*
Vous ouvrez *Vous venez*
Ils ouvrent *Ils viennent*
Elles ouvrent *Elles viennent*

cf. *couvrir* — to cover; cf. *tenir* — to hold;
  offrir — to offer;   *appartenir* — to belong;
  souffrir — to suffer.   *contenir* — to contain;
             obtenir — to obtain.

NB. Endings are those of an -ER Verb.

Voir — to see

Je vois
Tu vois
Il voit
Elle voit
Nous voyons
Vous voyez
Ils voient
Elles voient

Savoir — to know (a fact)

Je sais
Tu sais
Il sait
Elle sait
Nous savons
Vous savez
Ils savent
Elles savent

Pouvoir — to be able

Je peux
Tu peux
Il peut
Elle peut
Nous pouvons
Vous pouvez
Ils peuvent
Elles peuvent

Vouloir — to wish, to want

Je veux
Tu veux
Il veut
Elle veut
Nous voulons
Vous voulez
Ils veulent
Elles veulent

cf. *pleuvoir* — to rain (i.e. *il pleut*).

Valoir — to be worth

Je vaux
Tu vaux
Il vaut
Elle vaut
Nous valons
Vous valez
Ils valent
Elles valent

S'asseoir — to sit down

Je m'assieds
Tu t'assieds
Il s'assied
Elle s'assied
Nous nous asseyons
Vous vous asseyez
Ils s'asseyent
Elles s'asseyent

cf. *falloir* — to be necessary (i.e. *il faut*).

Grammar: Irregular Verbs

Devoir — to owe, to have to, must

Je dois
Tu dois
Il doit
Elle doit
Nous devons
Vous devez
Ils doivent
Elles doivent

Recevoir — to receive

Je reçois
Tu reçois
Il reçoit
Elle reçoit
Nous recevons
Vous recevez
Ils reçoivent
Elles reçoivent

Mourir — to die

Je meurs
Tu meurs
Il meurt
Elle meurt
Nous mourons
Vous mourez
Ils meurent
Elles meurent

Irregular -*RE* verbs:

Battre — to beat

Je bats ⎫
Tu bats ⎬ IRREGULAR
Il bat   ⎪
Elle bat ⎭
Nous battons
Vous battez
Ils battent
Elles battent

cf. mettre — to put;
  admettre — to admit;
  permettre — to allow;
  promettre — to promise.

Prendre — to take

Je prends
Tu prends
Il prend
Elle prend
Nous prenons ⎫
Vous prenez   ⎬ IRREGULAR
Ils prennent ⎪
Elles prennent⎭

cf. comprendre — to understand.

Naître — to be born

Je nais
Tu nais
Il naît
Elle naît
Nous naissons
Vous naissez
Ils naissent
Elles naissent

Paraître — to seem, to appear

Je parais
Tu parais
Il paraît
Elle paraît
Nous paraissons
Vous paraissez
Ils paraissent
Elles paraissent

cf. *connaître* — to know (a person or place); *reconnaître* — to recognize.

Boire — to drink

Je bois
Tu bois
Il boit
Elle boit
Nous buvons
Vous buvez
Ils boivent
Elles boivent

Croire — to think, to believe

Je crois
Tu crois
Il croit
Elle croit
Nous croyons
Vous croyez
Ils croient
Elles croient

Écrire — to write

J'écris
Tu écris
Il écrit
Elle écrit
Nous écrivons
Vous écrivez
Ils écrivent
Elles écrivent

Grammar: Irregular Verbs

Dire — to say, to tell

Je dis
Tu dis
Il dit
Elle dit
Nous disons
Vous dites
Ils disent
Elles disent

Lire — to read

Je lis
Tu lis
Il lit
Elle lit
Nous lisons
Vous lisez
Ils lisent
Elles lisent

'SAY NO EVIL, READ NO EVIL, NO LAUGHING!...

Rire — to laugh

Je ris
Tu ris
Il lit
Elle rit
Nous rions
Vous riez
Ils rient
Elles rient

Conduire — to lead, to drive

Je conduis
Tu conduis
Il conduit
Elle conduit
Nous conduisons
Vous conduisez
Ils conduisent
Elles conduisent

Suivre — to follow

Je suis
Tu suis
Il suit
Elle suit
Nous suivons
Vous suivez
Ils suivent
Elles suivent

Vivre — to live

Je vis
Tu vis
Il vit
Elle vit
Nous vivons
Vous vivez
Ils vivent
Elles vivent

Craindre — to fear

Je crains
Tu crains
Il craint
Elle craint
Nous craignons
Vous craignez
Ils craignent
Elles craignent

cf. *plaindre* — to pity;
  joindre — to join;
  peindre — to paint;
  atteindre — to attain;
  éteindre — to switch off.

Vaincre — to conquer

Je vaincs
Tu vaincs
Il vainc
Elle vainc
Nous vainquons
Vous vainquez
Ils vainquent
Elles vainquent

cf. *convaincre* — to convince

Coudre — to sew

Je couds
Tu couds
Il coud
Elle coud
Nous cousons
Vous cousez
Ils cousent
Elles cousent

'PERFECT TENTS HAVE TWO PARTS'...

Grammar: Perfect Tense

1.2 Perfect Tense – le passé composé or le parfait

The Perfect Tense always has <u>two</u> parts (cf. in English, I <u>have given</u>)

> ***Aide mémoire — think of it as an Equation***:
> The auxiliary (helper verb, i.e. *avoir* or *être*) + past participle = Perfect

Regular verbs:

-ER — -É (e.g., *donner* — *j'ai donné*)
-IR — -I (e.g., *finir* — *j'ai fini*)
-RE — -U (e.g., *vendre* — *j'ai vendu*)

Verbs conjugated with *Avoir*:

The vast majority of verbs have avoir as their auxiliary.

Irregular past participles of verbs with *Avoir*:

avoir	— to have	— eu
savoir	— to know	— su
pouvoir	—to be able	— pu
voir	— to see	— vu
pleuvoir	— to rain	— plu
vouloir	— to wish, to want	— voulu
devoir	— to owe; to have to	— dû
recevoir	— to receive	— reçu
courir	— to run	— couru
boire	—to drink	— bu
croire	— to think; to believe	— cru
connaître	— to know	— connu
paraître	— to appear	— paru
lire	— to read	— lu
rire	— to laugh	— ri
dire	— to say, to tell	— dit
écrire	— to write	— écrit
faire	— to make, to do	— fait

être	— to be	— été
mettre	— to put	— mis
prendre	— to take	— pris
couvrir	— to cover	— couvert
ouvrir	— to open	— ouvert
souffrir	— to suffer	— souffert
offrir	— to offer	— offert
conduire	— to lead	— conduit
vivre	— to live	— vécu
suivre	— to follow	— suivi
tenir	— to hold	— tenu
falloir	— to be necessary	— fallu
apercevoir	— to perceive	— aperçu
coudre	— to sew	— cousu
craindre	— to fear	— craint
joindre	— to join	— joint
peindre	— to paint	— peint

Verbs conjugated with *être* (13):

venir	—	to come	aller	—	to go
entrer	—	to come in	sortir	—	to go out
arriver	—	to arrive	partir	—	to depart; leave
rester	—	to stay	retourner	—	to return; go back
naître	—	to be born	mourir	—	to die
monter	—	to go up	descendre	—	go down
			tomber	—	to fall

NB. *Monter, descendre* and *sortir* take *avoir* with a direct object,
e.g.: *J'ai monté l'escalier* — I went up the stairs;
J'ai sort ma valise — I took out my suitcase.

Irregular past participles with *être*:

venir	—	venu
mourir	—	mort
naître	—	né

Grammar: Perfect Tense

Six compounds of the above 13 verbs:

revenir — to come back
devenir — to become
rentrer — to return (home)
ressortir — to go out again
remonter — to go up again
repartir — *to set off again*

All reflexive verbs go with *être*:

e.g., *elle s'est assise* — she (has) sat down.

Agreements:

With *avoir* the past participle must agree with, and only with, a preceding direct object (PDO),
e.g.: *Il les a apportés.*
Quelles tables avez-vous vendues?
With *être* the past participle must agree with the subject,
e.g.: *Elles sont sorties*.

1.3 Pluperfect Tense — *le plus-que-parfait*

Formation of pluperfect:

This is formed by taking the Imperfect of *avoir* or être instead of the present and adding the past participle,
e.g.: *Nous avions porté* — We had carried;
*Nous étions part*is — We had left.

1.4 Imperfect Tense — *l'imparfait*

The imperfect is a tense of description or repeated action in the past. It can be translated in four different ways, e.g.:
Il se levait — he got up, was getting up, used to get up, would get up;
Il se levait toujours à six heures — he always got up at six o'clock.

Aide-mémoire: Equation

stem of		imperfect endings			
1st person plural present tense	+	-ais -ais -ait	-ions -iez -aient	=	Imperfect
e.g: *nous donnons*	—	*je donnais*	—		I was giving
			—		I used to give
nous finissons	—	*je finissais*	—		I was finishing
			—		I used to finish
nous vendons	—	*je vendais*	—		I was selling
			—		I used to sell

NB. *Nous mangeons — je mangeais*
Nous commençons — je commençais

There is only one exception:

Être — j'étais — I was; I used to be

Grammar: Tenses

1.5 Future Tense – *le futur*

Aide-mémoire: Equation

Infinitive (reg.)	Present Tense			
Future stem (irreg. verbs) +	of *avoir* (-*av*)			
-*er*	-*ai*	-*ons*		
-*ir*	-*as*	-*ez*	=	Future
-*re*	-*a*	-*ont*		

NB. The future stem always ends in the letter *r*.

e.g.,   *Je donnerai*   —   I shall (will) give
          Je finirai   —   I shall finish
          je vendrai   —   I shall sell

Irregular verbs:

aller	—	to go	—	*j'irai*
venir	—	to come	—	*je viendrai*
tenir	—	to hold	—	*je tiendrai*
être	—	to be	—	*je serai*
faire	—	to do; to make	—	*je ferai*
avoir	—	to have	—	*j'aurai*
savoir	—	to know	—	*je saurai*
courir	—	to run	—	*je courrai*
mourir	—	to die	—	*je mourrai*
pouvoir	—	to be able	—	*je pourrai*
vouloir	—	to wish, to want	—	*je voudrai*
devoir	—	to owe, to have to	—	*je devrai*
recevoir	—	to receive	—	*je recevrai*
pleuvoir	—	to rain	—	*il pleuvra*
voir	—	to see	—	*je verrai*
envoyer	—	to send	—	*j'enverrai*
s'asseoir	—	to sit down	—	*je m'assiérai*
falloir	—	to be necessary	—	*il faudra*

Logical future:

Remember that French requires the future when futurity is implied, e.g.:
I will see you when you <u>come back</u> — *je te verrai quand tu <u>reviendras</u>.*

Use after the following conjunctions:

| Quand / Lorsque | = When | Aussitôt / Dès que | = As soon as |

Immediate Future:

The future tense can be avoided by using <u>aller + an infinitive</u>, e.g: *Je <u>vais</u> la <u>voir</u> jeudi* — I <u>will see</u> her.

1.6 Conditional Tense - *le conditionnel*

Aide mémoire: Equation

Infinitive (reg. verbs)   + imperfect   = Conditional
Future stem (irreg. verbs)   endings

    donner -ais   -ions
    finir   -ais   -iez
    vendre -ait   -aient

e.g.,   tomber — *je tomberais* — I would fall
         aller — *j'irais*   — I would go

THE IMPERATIVE...

1.7 Imperative Mood

The forms of the imperative are the 2nd person singular and plural, and the 1st person plural of the present tense, with the subject removed.

Donner	*Finir*	*Vendre*
donne! – give!	*finis!* – finish!	*vends!* – sell!
donnons! – let us give!	*finissons!* – let us finish!	*vendons* – let us sell!
donnez! – give!	*finissez!* – finish!	*vendez!* – sell!

NB. The 's' is dropped from the 2nd person singular if the last vowel is an 'e'.
This also applies to *aller*:
> *va!* – go!
> *allons!* – let us go!
> *allez!* – go!

There are only 3 exceptions:

Être	*Avoir*	*Savoir*
sois! – be!	*aie!* – have!	*sache!* – know!
soyons! – let us be!	*ayons!* – let us have!	*sachons!* – let us know!
soyez! – be!	*ayez!* – have!	*sachez!* – know!

Remember that in the case of the imperative affirmative (positive command) the object pronouns must follow the verb,
e.g.: – *Regardez-moi!* – look at me! *Assieds-toi!* ⎫
 – *Donnez-le-moi!* – give it to me! *Asseyez-vous!* ⎬ – sit down!
 ⎭

cf., – *Ne me regardez pas.* *Ne t'assieds pas.*
 – *Ne me le donnez pas.* *Ne vous asseyez pas.*

1.8 Infinitives

Where there are two verbs, the second is always put into the infinitive (cf. position of the object pronouns).

1.9 Present Participles

These are formed by adding -*ant* (-ing in English) to the stem of the first person plural present tense (i.e. the *nous* form), e.g.:

Nous finiss<u>ons</u> — finiss<u>ant</u> — finish<u>ing</u>

There are only 3 exceptions:

être	— *étant*	— being
avoir	— *ayant*	— having
savoir	— *sachant*	— knowing

Uses

(1) As an adjective (with agreement),
e.g., *des histoires amusantes* — amusing stories.
(2) With verbal force (no agreement),
e.g. *ayant faim il a vite mangé* — being hungry he ate quickly.
(3) With *en* meaning while, by, in, on (doing something),
e.g. *en se promenant dans la forêt* — while walking in the forest.

BUT do not over-use the present participle. Its uses are much more restricted than in English, i.e. I am giving = *je donne*.

Note the constructions *après avoir* and *après être* where a present participle is used in English,
e.g.: *Après avoir fermé la porte, le cambrioleur a sorti sa lampe de poche* — After shutting the door, the burglar took out his torch;

Après être sorti de la maison, il a refermé la porte — After leaving the house, he shut the door again.

Grammar: Verbs

1.10 Verbs followed by *à*

Verbs followed by *à* + infinitive:

apprendre à	—	to learn to
commencer à ⎫	—	to begin to
se mettre à ⎭		
continuer à	—	to continue to
inviter à	—	to invite to
réussir à	—	to manage to, to succeed in
se décider à	—	to decide to
se préparer à	—	to prepare to

Verbs followed by *à* + noun:

commander à	—	to order
conseiller à	—	to advise
défendre à	—	to forbid
demander à	—	to ask
désobéir à	—	to disobey
dire à	—	to tell
obéir à	—	to obey
ordonner à	—	to order
pardonner à	—	to forgive
permettre à	—	to allow, to permit
plaire à	—	to please
promettre à	—	to promise
rendre visite à	—	to visit (someone)
répondre à	—	to answer
résister à	—	to resist
ressembler à	—	to look like
servir à	—	to serve
téléphoner à	—	to ring, to phone

Note the following construction: *commander, conseiller, défendre, demander, dire, ordonner, permettre, promettre ... à quelqu'un de faire quelque chose*:
e.g., *Je dis à Jean de se lever* — I tell John to get up.
Sa mére lui permet de sortir — His mother lets him go out.

NB. *Répondez à la question* — *Répondez-y* — answer it.
Obéissez aux instructions — *Obéissez-y* — obey them.

1.11 Verbs followed by *de*

Verbs followed by *de* + infinitive:

cesser de	—	to cease to
continuer de	—	to continue to
décider de	—	to decide to
essayer de	—	to try to
finir de	—	to stop
offrir de	—	to offer to
oublier de	—	to forget to
refuser de	—	to refuse to
regretter de	—	to regret
s'arrêter de	—	to stop

Verbs followed by *de* + noun:

partir de	—	to leave
s'approcher de	—	to approach
se douter de	—	to suspect
s'occuper de	—	to take care of
se servir de	—	to use
se souvenir de	—	to remember
se tromper de	—	to make a mistake

Note the following examples:

Servez-vous-en	—	use it
Elle s'en occupe	—	she is looking after it
Je m'en souviendrai	—	I shall remember it
Je me suis trompé de cahier	—	I have brought the wrong exercise book
Elle s'est trompée de route	—	she took the wrong route

Jouer de and *jouer à*:

Jouer de is used with musical instruments,
   e.g: *Je joue du trombone, du violon et de la guitare.*

Jouer à is used with games and sports,
   e.g: *Je joue au tennis et aux échecs.*

Grammar: Verbs

Penser de* and *penser à*:
Penser de means '*to think*' in the sense of 'to have an opinion',
  e.g: Que pensez-vous de lui? — What do you think of him?

Penser à means 'to think' as a mental process,
  e.g: *À quoi pensez-vous?* — what are you thinking about?

1.12 *Entrer dans*

NB. *Le garçon est entré dans la salle de classe* — the boy entered the classroom.

1.13 Some French Verbs which include the English Preposition

approuver	—	to approve of
attendre	—	to wait for
chercher	—	to look for
demander	—	to ask for
écouter	—	to listen to
envoyer chercher	—	to send for
habiter	—	to live in
payer	—	to pay for
regarder	—	to look at
soigner	—	to care for
viser	—	to aim at

e.g., *J'attends le facteur* — I am waiting for the postman.

1.14 The Passive Voice

Formation: *être* in any of its tenses + past participle of a transitive verb (A transitive verb is one which can take a direct object), e.g.:

Present	—	*je suis vu(e)*	—	I am seen
Perfect	—	*jai été vu(e)*	—	I have been seen
Imperfect	—	*j'étais vu(e)*	—	I was seen
Future	—	*je serai vu(e)*	—	I will be seen

NB. Because *être* is used, the past participle must agree with the subject.

'By' after a verb in the passive is usually translated by *par*, e.g.:
Il sera puni par le proviseur — he will be punished by the headmaster.

But **note**:

Il était accompagné de ses enfants — he was accompanied by his children; *elle est aimée de tout le monde* — she is liked by everyone.

Avoidance of the Passive

The passive voice is used less frequently in French than it is in English, and there are two common ways of avoiding it:

(1) By making the sentence active with '*on*' as the subject, e.g.:
on l'a arrêté — he was arrested;
ici on parle anglais — English (is) spoken here;
on lui a fait payer une amende — he was forced to pay a fine.

NB. The indirect object cannot be turned round to become the subject of the French passive construction, as we often do in English, e.g.:
on m'a donné un cadeau — I was given a present;
on lui a dit la vérité — He was told the truth.

(2) By using a reflexive verb, e.g.:
je m'appelle Jacques — I am called James.
Comment se dit-il en français? — How is that said in French?
Comment s'est-il habillé? — How was he dressed?

2 NOUNS

2.1 Gender of Nouns

Words ending in:	Usually	Common Exceptions
-age	Masculine	la page; la plage; la rage; la cage; la nage; une image
-aire	Masculine	
-al	Masculine	
-ance	Feminine	
-cycle	Masculine	
-eau	Masculine	l'eau; la peau
-ée	Feminine	le lycée; le musée
-ème	Masculine	
-ence	Feminine	le silence
-ent	Masculine	la dent
-er	Masculine	la mer
-et	Masculine	la forêt
-ette	Feminine	le squelette
-eu	Masculine	
-eur	Masculine (if person)	
-eur	Feminine	le bonheur; le malheur; l'honneur; (if not) le moteur; le radiateur
-euse	Feminine	
-isme	Masculine	
-ment	Masculine	la jument
-(m)ure	Feminine	
-ou	Masculine	
-tion	Feminine	

NOTE: la feuille — leaf   le portefeuille — wallet
la monnaie — change   le porte-monnaie — purse
la pluie — rain   le parapluie — umbrella
la chute — fall   le parachute — parachute

Nouns with 2 genders:

<u>Masculine</u>

le chèvre — goat's cheese
le livre — book
le manche — handle

le page — page boy
le poêle — stove
le poste — post, position
le somme — nap
le tour — trick, turn, tour
le vague — vagueness
le vase — vase

<u>Feminine</u>

la chèvre — goat
la livre — pound
la manche — sleeve;
la Manche — English Channel
la page — page
la poêle — frying pan
la poste — post, post office
la somme — sum of money
la tour — tower
la vague — wave
la vase — river mud

2.2 Plurals of Nouns

To make a noun plural we usually add 's', but there are some exceptions:

<u>Words Ending in</u>:	<u>Plural</u>	<u>Examples</u>
-al	-aux	les animaux; les journaux; les chevaux
-eau	-x	les bateaux; les cadeaux; les châteaux
-eu	-x	les jeux; les feux; les cheveux
-s	No change	les bras; les bois
-x	No change	les voix
-z	No change	les nez
-ou	-s	les tr<u>ou</u>s

Grammar: Nouns

But seven only take a plural in 'x', viz:

le bijou	—	jewel	*le caillou*	—	pebble
le chou	—	cabbage	*le genou*	—	knee
le hibou	—	owl	*le joujou*	—	toy
le pou	—	louse			

NOTE also:

un oeil bleu	—	*des yeux bleus*
le travail	—	*les travaux*
la grand-mère	—	*les grands-mères*
le ciel	—	*les cieux*
monsieur	—	*messieurs*
madame	—	*mesdames*

3 PRONOUNS

3.1 Personal Pronouns

		Conjunctive (Weak)			(Strong)
Subject	Direct Obj.	Indirect Obj.		Reflexive Obj.	Disjunctive
1 *Je* - I	*Me* - Me	*Me* - To Me		*Me* - Myself	*Moi*
2 *Tu* - You	*Te* - You	*Te* - To You		*Te* - Yourself	*Toi*
3 *Il* - He	*Le* - Him	*Lui* -	To Him	*Se* - Himself	*Lui*
Elle - She	*La* - Her		To Her	Herself	*Elle*
1 *Nous* - We	*Nous* - Us	*Nous* - To Us		*Nous* - Ourselves	*Nous*
2 *Vous* - You	*Vous* - You	*Vous* - To You		*Vous* - Yourselves	*Vous*
3 *Ils* - They	*Les* - Them	*Leur* - To Them		*Se* - Themselves	*Eux*
Elles					*Elles*
On - One				*Se* - Oneself	*Soi*

NB. y = there   A preposition + noun is often replaced by y, e.g: *Il entre dans la maison — Il y entre.*

En = some, any, of it, of them, from it, from them.
De + Noun replaced by *En*,
   e.g: *J'ai besoin <u>de votre aide</u> — J'<u>en</u> ai besoin.*
No agreement with *En*!

Order of object pronouns:

me					
te	*le*	*lui*			
se	*la*	*leur*	*y*	*en*	Verb
nous	*les*				
vous		(Like a football team's formation)

The above order is followed when there is more than one object pronoun in a sentence.

ORDER OF PRONOUNS (FOOTBALL TEAM FORMATION)

Position of object pronouns in a sentence:

The object pronoun comes <u>before the verb</u>:

(a) When there is <u>one</u> verb in a sentence in the Perfect tense the object pronoun comes <u>immediately before the auxiliary verb</u>, e.g: *il l'a porté.*

(b) When there are <u>two</u> verbs in a sentence the second is in the infinitive, and the object pronoun comes <u>immediately before the infinitive,</u> e.g: *nous allons le trouver.*

NB. There is <u>one</u> case where the object pronoun <u>follows the verb</u>, i.e. a positive command. This is the case where you are telling someone to do something, e.g: *Regardez-moi!; ouvrez-les!*

Grammar: Pronouns

In this case *me* and *te* become *moi* and *toi,* and one puts a hyphen between the verb and pronoun. The order is thus:

		-moi		
		-toi		
	-le	-nous		
Verb	-la	-vous	-y	-en
	-les	-lui		
		-leur		(English word order)

But *me* and *te* do not change before y or *en,* e.g:
assieds-t'y — sit there; *prétez-m'en* — lend me some.

Use of disjunctive pronouns:

(1) <u>After a preposition,</u> e.g: *avec eux* — with them.
(2) <u>After *c'est* and *ce sont*,</u> e.g: *c'est moi* — it is I.
(3) <u>After *que* in a comparison,</u> e.g:
    je suis plus grand que toi — I am taller than you.
(4) <u>For emphasis,</u> e.g: *vous, vous étes stupide*.
(5) <u>Replacing a noun standing on its own,</u> e.g:
    Qui a dit cela? Lui? Non, elle.

3.2 Interrogative Pronouns

These replace interrogative adjective *quel* etc. + noun.

	<u>Masculine</u>	<u>Feminine</u>
Singular	*lequel?* — Which one?	*Laquelle?* — Which one?
Plural	*lesquels?* — Which ones?	*Lesquelles?* — Which ones?

3.3 Demonstrative Pronouns

These replace demonstrative adjective *ce, cette, ces* + noun:

	Masculine	Feminine
Singular	c*elui* — This one, the one	c*elle* — This one, the one
Plural	c*eux* — These, those	c*elles* — These, those

They must be followed by either:
    (a) *qui; que; dont;*
or (b) *de;*
or (c) *-ci; -là.*

NB. 'The former' — *celui-là; celle-là*, etc;
     'The latter' — *celui-ci; celle-ci*, etc.

3.4 Relative Pronouns

Subject	*qui*	— who, which
Direct Object	*que(qu')*	— whom, which
Possessive	*dont*	— whose, of whom
After Preposition	*lequel, laquelle, lesquels, lesquelles* — which

e.g.: *C'est un garçon <u>qui</u> a beaucoup d'amis;*
     Le garçon, <u>que</u> je connais, a beaucoup d'amis;
     Le livre, <u>dont</u> vous avez besoin, est sur la table;
     Le stylo, <u>avec lequel</u> il écrit, coûte cher.

NB. *à + lequel* — *auquel; de + lequel* — *duquel*
     à + lesquels — *auxquels; de + lesquels* — *desquels*

THE KEY WORD!

Grammar: Pronouns

How to distinguish between *QUI* and *QUE*:

Qui (subject) and *que* (object) can both mean <u>which</u>.
BUT remember this golden rule, and you will avoid errors:

qui + Verb; *que* + Noun or Pronoun, e.g.:

La robe de fête, <u>que</u> sa mère a achetée, et <u>qu'</u>elle aime le mieux, est celle <u>qui</u> a été déchirée.

3.5 Possessive Pronouns

These replace possessive adjectives *mon, ma, mes*, etc. + noun:

	Singular		Plural	
<u>Masculine</u>		<u>Feminine</u>	<u>Masculine</u>	<u>Feminine</u>
le mien	— mine	*la mienne*	*les miens*	*les miennes*
le tien	— yours	*la tienne*	*les tiens*	*les tiennes*
le sien	— his, hers	*la sienne*	*les siens*	*les siennes*
le nôtre	— ours	*la nôtre*	*les nôtres*	*les nôtres*
le vôtre	— yours	*la vôtre*	*les vôtres*	*les vôtres*
le leur	— theirs	*la leur*	*les leurs*	*les leurs*

4 ADJECTIVES

4.1 Agreement of Adjective with Noun

In the normal way adjectives form their feminine by adding -*e*, their masculine plural by adding -*s*, and their feminine plural by adding -*es*. Thus:

	Singular	Plural
Masculine	-	-s
Feminine	-e	-es

BUT those adjectives ending in a silent -*e* do not add another -*e* in the feminine: they remain the same, e.g: *un livre rouge; une voiture rouge*.

RULE: Never write two silent *e*'s together. The first must always have an accent, e.g., *la poupée; il l'a créée*.

Irregular agreements:

Masculine			Feminine	
premier	[er]	— first	première	[ère]
curieux	[x]	— curious	curieuse	[se]
actif	[f]	— active	active	[ve]
criminel	[el]	— criminal	criminelle	[elle]
parisien	[en]	— parisian	parisienne	[enne]
muet	[et]	— dumb	muette	[ette]
bon	[on]	— good	bonne	[onne]
gras	[as]	— fat	grasse	[asse]
pareil	[eil]	— similar	pareille	[eille]
blanc		— white	blanche	
long		— long	longue	
doux		— sweet	douce	
faux		— false	fausse	
gros		— big	grosse	
épais		— thick	épaisse	
sot		— foolish	sotte	
gentil		— kind	gentille	
sec		— dry	sèche	
favori		— favourite	favorite	
frais		— fresh	fraîche	
public		— public	publique	

Grammar: Adjectives

BUT:

Masculine			Feminine
secret	—	secret	*secrète*
complet	—	complete	*complète*
discret	—	discreet	*discrète*
inquiet	—	anxious	*inquiète*

Some adjectives have a distinct form in the masculine singular before a noun beginning with a vowel or silent h.

Singular

Masculine			Masculine before vowel	Feminine
beau	—	beautiful	*bel*	*belle*
nouveau	—	new	*nouvel*	*nouvelle*
vieux	—	old	*vieil*	*vieille*
fou	—	mad	*fol*	*folle*
mou	—	soft	*mol*	*molle*

Plural

Masculine			Feminine		
beau / *bel*	—	*beaux;*	*belle*	—	*belles*
vieux / *vieil*	—	*vieux;*	*vieille*	—	*vieilles*

Aide-mémoire: Remember that an old woman has two *eyes*,
e.g: *La vieille* — the old woman;
　　La veille — the eve, preceding day.

4.2 Position of Adjective in relation to Noun

The vast majority of adjectives follow the noun,
e.g.: *un mur <u>bas</u>*   — a low wall
    une porte <u>verte</u>   — a green door
    des histoires <u>amusantes</u>   — amusing stories

The following adjectives usually *precede the noun:*

bon — good	beau — beautiful
mauvais — bad	joli — pretty
petit — small	vilain — mean; ugly
grand — big; great	méchant — naughty; wicked
gros — big; stout	gentil — kind
vieux — old	haut — high
jeune — young	vaste — vast
nouveau — new	meilleur — better
long — long	ancien — former, ex.
premier — first	dernier — final

4.3 Interrogative Adjectives

	Masculine	Feminine
Singular:	*Quel?* — Which? What?	*Quelle?* — Which? etc.
Plural:	*Quels?* — Which?	*Quelles?* — Which?

4.4 Demonstrative Adjectives

	Masculine	Masculine before vowel	Feminine
Singular	ce — *this, that*	cet — *this, that*	cette — *this, that*
Plural		ces — *these, those*	

Grammar: Adverbs

4.5 Possessive Adjectives

		Masculine	Feminine	Plural
mon	—	my	*ma*	*mes*
ton	—	your	*ta*	*tes*
son	—	his, her	*sa*	*ses*
notre	—	our	*notre*	*nos*
votre	—	your	*votre*	*vos*
leur	—	their	*leur*	*leurs*

5 ADVERBS

5.1 Formation

To form the adverb from the adjective add *-ment* (= -ly in English) if the adjective ends in a vowel; e.g., *stupide* → *stupide*ment — stupid*ly*.

If the adjective ends in a consonant then make it feminine first; e.g., *dernier* → *dernièrement* — lastly.

If the adjective ends in *-nt* then change to *-m* before you add *-ment*; e.g., *courant* → *coura*mment — fluently;
violent → *viole*mment — violently.

5.2 Common Irregular Adverbs

lent	→	*lentement*	—	slowly
vite	→	*vite*	—	quickly, fast
bon	→	*bien*	—	well
mauvais	→	*mal*	—	badly
petit	→	*peu*	—	little
meilleur	→	*mieux*	—	better
gai	→	*gaiement*	—	gaily
fou	→	*follement*	—	madly
mou	→	*mollement*	—	softly
gentil	→	*gentiment*	—	kindly
énorme	→	*énormément*	—	enormously
précis	→	*précisément*	—	precisely
profond	→	*profondément*	—	deeply

6 PREPOSITIONS

6.1 Some Important Prepositions

(1)	sur	— on	(15)	pendant	— during; for
(2)	sous	— under	(16)	depuis	— since; for
(3)	derrière	— behind	(17)	vers	— towards
(4)	devant	— in front of	(18)	contre	— against
(5)	avec	— with	(19)	près de	— near to
(6)	sans	— without	(20)	loin de	— far from
(7)	avant	— before	(21)	par	— through; by
(8)	après	— after	(22)	à travers	— through; across
(9)	dans	— in; into	(23)	chez	— at (to) the house of
(10)	à	— to; at; in	(24)	parmi	— among
(11)	en	— in; to	(25)	malgré	— in spite of, despite
(12)	de	— of; from	(26)	à côté de	— next to
(13)	entre	— between	(27)	au-dessous de	— below
(14)	pour	— for; in order to	(28)	au-dessus de	— above

NB. *To, at* or *in* a town = à;
e.g., *à Paris; à Londres; à Edimbourg; à Douvres; au Havre.*

To or *in* a country = en;
e.g., *en France; en Angleterre.*

BUT with masculine countries (those not ending in a silent -*e*) use *au; aux*.
In a county = *dans le*; e.g., <u>dans le</u> *Devon*. Note the exception <u>en</u> *Cornouailles* = in Cornwall.

Grammar: Prepositions

6.2 Countries

Some masculine countries:

au	Canada	—	in Canada
au	Portugal	—	in Portugal
au	Danemark	—	in Denmark
au	Japon	—	in Japan
au	Pays de Galles	—	in Wales
aux	États Unis	—	in the United States
aux	Antilles	—	in the West Indies
aux	Pays-Bas	—	in the Netherlands

Some feminine countries:

en	France	—	in France
en	Angleterre	—	in England
en	Écosse	—	in Scotland
en	Irlande	—	in Ireland
en	Italie	—	in Italy
en	Espagne	—	in Spain
en	Belgique	—	in Belgium
en	Hollande	—	in Holland
en	Suisse	—	in Switzerland
en	Allemagne	—	in Germany
en	Autriche	—	in Austria
en	Norvège	—	in Norway
en	Suède	—	in Sweden
en	Finlande	—	in Finland
en	Russie	—	in Russia
en	Grèce	—	in Greece
en	Inde	—	in India
en	Chine	—	in China

6.3 The Continents

en	Europe	—	in Europe
en	Asie	—	in Asia
en	Amérique	—	in America
en	Afrique	—	in Africa
en	Australie	—	in Australia

6.4 Prepositional Phrases

There is considerable subtlety in the way prepositions are used in French, and the literal translation must often be avoided. The following prepositional phrases should prove both useful and enlightening.

au soleil	—	in the sun
sous la pluie	—	in the rain
à l'ombre	—	in the shade
par un temps pareil	—	in such weather
de cette manière	—	in this way
à la campagne	—	in the countryside
en ville	—	in town
de nos jours	—	in our time, nowadays
sous le règne de	—	in the reign of
la dame aux lunettes	—	the lady in the glasses
le plus petit garçon de la classe	—	the smallest boy in the class
pendant les vacances	—	in the holidays
dans une ferme	—	on a farm
dans une île	—	on an island
au tableau noir	—	on the blackboard
la carte pend au mur	—	the map is hanging on the wall
par terre	—	on the ground
par une journée d'été	—	on a summer's day
par politesse	—	out of politeness
huit sur dix	—	eight out of ten
en bois	—	made (out) of wood
en brique	—	made (out) of brick
en pierre	—	made (out) of stone
en verre	—	made (out) of glass
un sac en plastique	—	a plastic bag
de temps en temps	—	from time to time
deux fois par an	—	twice a year
à pied	—	on foot
à vélo; à bicyclette	—	by bike
en auto; en voiture	—	by car
en train	—	by train
en bateau	—	by boat
en avion	—	by plane
vers une heure	—	about one o'clock

aux yeux bruns — with brown eyes
il est fâché contre moi — he is angry with me
il a bu dans le verre — he drank from the glass
il l'a pris dans le tiroir — he took it out of the drawer
il l'a pris sur le rayon — he took it off the shelf
il a changé d'avis — he changed his mind
il me parle en ami — he speaks to me as a friend

7 NEGATIVES

ne ... pas	—	not	
ne ... pas du tout	—	not at all	
ne ... plus	—	no more; no longer	
ne ... rien	—	nothing	
ne ... jamais	—	never	
ne ... que	—	only; nothing but; except for	
ne ... personne	—	no-one; nobody	
ne ... ni ... ni	—	neither ... nor	
ne ... guère	—	scarcely; hardly	
ne ... aucun / *ne ... nul(le)*	—	no, none	(literary)
ne ... nulle part	—	nowhere	
ne ... point	—	not (at all)	(literary)

NB. *Je n'ai rien dit* — I have said <u>nothing</u>, **but** *je n'ai vu personne* — I have seen <u>no one:</u> i.e. *personne* and *nulle part* must follow the past participle.

Rien and *personne* can also be the subject of a sentence, e.g.:
Rien n'est perdu — <u>nothing</u> is lost;
Personne n'est arrivé — <u>nobody</u> has arrived.
In this case *rien* and *personne* are not complete without *ne* before the verb.

8 USES OF *DE*

The partitive article (*du, de la, de l', des*) is shortened to *de* or *d'*:

(1) After a negative, e.g., *Je n'ai pas de pommes*.

(2) After an expression of quantity, e.g., *Il a beaucoup de livres*.

beaucoup	— much, many, a lot	*combien*	— how much, how many
trop	— too much; too many	*assez*	— enough
tant	— so much, so many	*peu*	— little

(3) Before an adjective + noun in the plural,
e.g.: *Il porte de grands cahiers*.
But *Il porte des cahiers rouges*,
because it is a noun + adjective in the plural.

9 IDIOMS

9.1 Idioms with *Avoir*

avoir froid	—	to be cold
avoir chaud	—	to be hot
avoir faim	—	to be hungry
avoir soif	—	to be thirsty
avoir raison	—	to be right
avoir tort	—	to be wrong
avoir peur	—	to be afraid
avoir sommeil	—	to be sleepy
avoir honte	—	to be ashamed
avoir lieu	—	to take place
avoir l'air	—	to seem
avoir besoin de	—	to need
avoir h?te de	—	to be eager to
avoir envie de	—	to want
avoir mal à	—	to have something wrong with

NB.	*Nous avons chaud*	—	We are hot
	Il fait chaud	—	It is hot weather
	L'eau est chaude	—	The water is hot

Grammar: Idioms

9.2 Idioms with *Faire*

Il fait beau (temps)	—	It is fine weather
Il fait mauvais (temps)	—	It is bad weather
Il fait chaud	—	It is hot
Il fait froid	—	It is cold
Il fait frais	—	It is cool
Il fait jour	—	It is daylight
Il fait nuit	—	It is dark
Il fait sombre	—	It is dark
Il fait du soleil	—	It is sunny
Il fait du vent	—	It is windy
Il fait du brouillard	—	It is foggy
Il fait de l'orage	—	It is thundering
Il fait un temps couvert	—	It is overcast; cloudy
Il fait un temps affreux	—	The weather is awful
Il fait un temps superbe	—	The weather is splendid
Cela ne fait rien	—	It doesn't matter

9.3 *Venir* de + infinitive

Venir de + infinitive = to have just done something.
It is used in the <u>present</u> or the <u>imperfect</u> tenses,
e.g.: *Ils <u>viennent</u> <u>de</u> sortir* — They have just gone out;
      Ils <u>venaient</u> <u>de</u> sortir — They had just gone out.

In English we use the <u>perfect</u> or the <u>pluperfect</u> respectively.

9.4 Tenses with *depuis*

Similarly *depuis* (since) used with the <u>present</u> or the <u>imperfect</u> translates an action or state in the past, which is still going on at the present time,
e.g.: <u>*Ils sont*</u> *ici <u>depuis</u> une semaine* —
      <u>They have been</u> here <u>for</u> a week.   (English perfect)

      <u>*Ils étaient*</u> *ici <u>depuis</u> une semaine* —
      <u>They had been</u> here for a week.   (English pluperfect)

9.5 Être en train de

Être en train de — to be occupied in, to be in the middle of,
e.g.:   Je suis en train de faire mes devoirs —
        I am engaged in doing my homework.

Note also: Être sur le point de — to be about to,
e.g.:   J'étais sur le point de me coucher —
        I was about to go to bed.

9.6 C'est; Il est

As a general rule, *c'est* refers back and *il est* refers forward,
e.g.:   Il est difficile de comprendre la lettre.
        Il a gagné le tournoi; c'est difficile à faire.

Use *c'est* with a noun or pronoun,
e.g.:   c'est un homme.; c'est lui.

NB.   Il est professeur. (Omit the indefinite article)
        C'est un professeur.

PART B
MISCELLANEOUS INFORMATION

10.1 Distinguish between...

(1)	*aider*	—	to assist
(2)	*assister à*	—	to attend
(3)	*attendre*	—	to wait for
(4)	*entendre*	—	to hear
(5)	*écouter*	—	to listen to
(1)	*montrer*	—	to show; to point to
(2)	*monter*	—	to climb up
(3)	*mentir*	—	to (tell a) lie
(1)	*retourner*	—	to return (go back)
(2)	*revenir*	—	to return (come back)
(3)	*rentrer*	—	to return (home)
(4)	*rendre*	—	to return (give back)
(1)	*savoir*	—	to know (a fact)
(2)	*connaître*	—	to know (a person or place)

10.2 *L'Alphabet français*

To know and pronounce the French alphabet is essential! The following guide may help you to learn and remember it:

(✓) F, L, M, N, O, S, Z are similar to their English counterparts.
(x) B, C, D, G, P, T, V, W rhyme with the English word 'bay'.
    I, J rhyme with each other.
    K, R sound like 'car' and air'.

Thus:
	A		E		I ⎫ rhyme	M ✓	Q	U	Y (*i grec*)
	B	x	F	✓	j ⎭	N ✓	R (air)	V x	Z ✓
	C	x	G	x	K (car)	O ✓	S ✓	W x	
	D	x	H		L ✓	P x	T x	X	

ACCENT ON A GRAVE SITUATION

10.3 *Les Accents*

(é) — *accent aigu* (acute), e.g. *l'été*
(è) — *accent grave* (grave), e.g. *le père*
(ê) — *accent circonflexe* (circumflex), e.g. *être*
(ë) — *tréma* (diaeresis), e.g. *Noël*
(ç) — *accent cédille* (cedilla), e.g. *le garçon*

NB. Circumflex usually indicates an s has been omitted, e.g. *château* – castle. But *otage* (hostage) has no circumflex.
Cedilla softens a hard c (*Nous commençons*).
Diaeresis indicates that two vowels should be pronounced independently of one another (contrast diphthong *la sœur*).

10.4 Days – *Les Jours de la Semaine*

lundi	—	Monday
mardi	—	Tuesday
mercredi	—	Wednesday
jeudi	—	Thursday
vendredi	—	Friday
samedi	—	Saturday
dimanche	—	Sunday

DAYS OF THE WEEK

(Moon, Mars, Mercury, Jupiter, Venus, Saturn, Lord's Day)

10.5 Months — *Les Mois de l'Année*

janvier	—	January
février	—	February
mars	—	March
avril	—	April
mai	—	May
juin	—	June
juillet	—	July
août	—	August
septembre	—	September
octobre	—	October
novembre	—	November
décembre	—	December

10.6 Seasons — *Les Quatre Saisons de l'Année*

le printemps	—	Spring	<u>*au*</u> *printemps*	—	<u>in</u> Spring
l'été (m)	—	Summer	<u>*en*</u> *été*	—	<u>in</u> Summer
l'automne (m or f)	—	Autumn	<u>*en*</u> *automne*	—	<u>in</u> Autumn
l'hiver (m)	—	Winter	<u>*en*</u> *hiver*	—	<u>in</u> Winter

10.7 Numbers — *Les Nombres Cardinaux*

1. *un; une*	13. *treize*	50. *cinquante*	
2. *deux*	14. *quatorze*	60. *soixante*	
3. *trois*	15. *quinze*	70. *soixante-dix*	
4. *quatre*	16. *seize*	71. *soixante et onze*	
5. *cinq*	17. *dix-sept*	80. *quatre-vingts*	
6. *six*	18. *dix-huit*	81. *quatre-vingt-un*	
7. *sept*	19. *dix-neuf*	90. *quatre-vingt-dix*	
8. *huit*	20. *vingt*	100. *cent*	
9. *neuf*	21. *vingt et un*	200. *deux cents*	
10. *dix*	22. *vingt-deux*	201. *deux cent un* (NB. no s in cent)	
11. *onze*	30. *trente*	1000. *mille*	
12. *douze*	40. *quarante*	2000. *deux mille*	

Note also:
dizaine — (about) 10; *vingtaine* — (about) 20; a score
douzaine — (about) 12; dozen *quarantaine* — (about) 40; quarantine
quinzaine — (about) 15; fortnight *centaine* — (about) 100

Les nombres ordinaux:

1st	—	*premier*	5th	— *cinquième*
2nd	—	*deuxième; second*	9th	— *neuvième*
3rd	—	*troisième*	21st	— *vingt et unième*
4th	—	*quatrième*	1000th	— *millième*

10.8 Date — *La Date*

But dates are written with cardinal numbers,
e.g.: *vendredi, le vingt-six mars.*

Except for the first of the month,
e.g.: *jeudi, le premier août.*

NB. Remember DATES MUST BE WRITTEN IN small letters.

10.9 Time — *l'heure*

Note the following examples:

Il est une heure cinq	— It is five past one
Il est deux heures dix	— It is ten past two
Il est trois heures et quart	— It is quarter past three
Il est quatre heures vingt-cinq	— It is twenty five past four
Il est cinq heures et demie	— It is half past five
Il est six heures moins vingt	— It is twenty to six
Il est sept heures moins le quart	— It is quarter to seven
Il est huit heures du matin	— It is eight o'clock in the morning
Il est deux heures de l'après-midi	— It is two o'clock in the afternoon
Il est neuf heures du soir	— It is nine o'clock in the evening
Il est midi	— It is midday
Il est midi et quart	— It is quarter past twelve (noon)
Il est midi vingt	— It is twenty past twelve (12.20 p.m.)
Il est midi et demi	— It is half past twelve (12.30 p.m.)
Il est minuit moins le quart	— It is quarter to twelve (11.45 p.m.)
Il est minuit moins cinq	— It is five to twelve (11.55 p.m.)
Il est minuit	— It is midnight
Il est minuit et demi	— It is half past twelve (12.30 a.m.)

10.10 Some Linguistic Subtleties

Note the following points:

Oui means 'yes', but use *si* when contradicting,
e.g.: *'Vous n'aimez pas le repas?' 'Si.'* (= Yes, I do.)

Merci can mean 'No thank you' in answer to a direct question,
e.g.: *'Encore du vin?' 'Merci, pas pour moi.'*

(Be careful how you say *merci*, or you may not receive the second helping you wanted!)

Le Français = Frenchman; *le français* = the French language.
(i.e. capital letter F for the person; lower-case (small) letter for the language.)

Use of the definite article with parts of the body,
e.g.: *Il ouvre la bouche* — he opens his mouth;
Je me suis cassé la jambe — I have broken my leg.

Logical French use of singular for English plural,
e.g.: *Ils secouaient la tête* — they shook their heads;
Ils se donnaient la main — they were holding hands (= one hand each).

Note also: *le pantalon* — trousers, a pair of trousers
le pyjama — pyjamas

Slight differences in spelling:

French		English
adresse	—	address
littérature	—	literature
mariage	—	marriage
millionnaire	—	millionaire
tarif	—	tariff
indépendant	—	independent
par exemple	—	for example

PART C
11 COMPREHENSION

11.1 Question Words

(1)	*Pourquoi?*	—	Why? (Answer usually requires *parce que*)
(2)	*Où?*	—	Where?
(3)	*Quand?*	—	When?
(4)	*Comment?*	—	How? What? What ... like?
(5)	*Combien?*	—	How much? How many?
(6)	*Qui?*	—	Who?
(7)	*Que?*	—	What?
(8)	*Qu'est-ce que?*	—	What?
(9)	*Est-ce que?*	—	Is it that?
(10)	*Quel + noun?*	—	Which? What?
(11)	*De quelle couleur?*	—	What colour?
(12)	*Depuis quand?*	—	How long?
(13)	*À quoi sert?*	—	To what use? For what purpose?

11.2 Important Questions

1. Q. *Comment vous appelez-vous?*
   A. *Je m'appelle Michel Blanc.*

2. Q. *Quel âge avez-vous?*
   A. *J'ai treize ans.*

3. Q. *Où habitez-vous?*
   A. *J'habite (à) Paris.*

4. Q. *Comment allez-vous?*
   A. *Je vais très bien, merci.*

5. Q. *Avez-vous des frères ou des sœurs?*
   A. *Oui, j'ai un frère et une sœur.*
      Non, je suis fils/fille enfant unique.

6. Q. *Quelle est votre matière préférée?*
   A. *J'adore le français/l'histoire/les maths.*

7. Q. *Quel est votre sport préféré?*
   A. *J'aime jouer au tennis/C'est le foot.*

8. Q. *Combien d'élèves y a-t-il dans votre classe?*
   A. *Il y en a vingt-cinq.*
9. Q. *Quelle heure est-il?*
   A. *Il est deux heures et demie.*
10. Q. *Quel temps fait-il?*
    A. *Il fait beau.*
11. Q. *Quel jour sommes-nous aujourd'hui?*
    A. *Aujourd'hui nous sommes lundi.*
12. Q. *Quelle est la date aujourd'hui?*
    A. *La date est mardi, le quatorze juillet.*

PART D
12 PRONUNCIATION
12.1 Sounds

Here are some rules which should help your spelling.

The following letters or combinations of letters are all pronounced rather like A, the first letter of the English alphabet:

1) -er   cf. *donner*
2) -ez   cf. *vous donnez*
3) -é   cf. *j'ai donné*
4) -ai   cf. *j'ai; je donnerai*
5) -et   (= and)

The following letters or combinations of letters are pronounced [e] as in the English word 'red:

1) -es   cf. *tu es*
2) -est   cf. *il est*
3) -ais   cf. *je donnais* (imperfect tense)
4) -ait   cf. *il finirait* (conditional tense)
5) -aient cf. *ils vendaient*
6) ê   cf *être; la fenêtre*
7) è   cf. *le père* (long vowel sound)

N.B. Distinguish carefully between *et* (and): *est* (is).

[i] The French letter I is pronounced like the English letter e, e.g., *il dit*.

[ou] The letters ou are pronounced like the English word 'boo', e.g., *un sou; le bout*.

[au] The letters au and eau are pronounced like the English word 'oh!', e.g., *au; chaud*.

[eau] e.g., *l'eau; beau; le chapeau*.

[eu]	The letters eu are pronounced as in French word '*neuf*'. Exception: *J'ai eu* (u sound).
[eur]	The letters eur are pronounced like the English word 'sir' but with a guttural re, e.g., *leur*; *l'heure*.
[oi]	The letters oi are pronounced as in the English word 'won', e.g., *un oiseau*; *le bois*.
[u]	This represents a combination of oo and ee, e.g., *du*; *le but*; *sur*. One forms the lips to say oo and tries to say the ee sound.

Contrast the difference between:

(1) *au-dessus* — above   (1) *le but* — goal; aim
(2) *au-dessous* — below   (2) *le bout* — end

[h]	NEVER PRONOUNCE the h, e.g., *un homme*.
[th]	Pronounced as t, e.g., *le théâtre*.
[s]	Pronounced Z (in middle of word), e.g., *le vase*; *la maison*. Pronounced S (at beginning), e.g., *sortir*.
[ss]	Pronounced s (in middle of word), e.g., *ressortir*.
[l]	Pronounced l, e.g., *un élève*; but note *le fils* (rhymes with English 'peace').
[ll]	Sometimes - ll, e.g., *la ville*; *le village*; *belle*. Sometimes silent, e.g., *la fille* (as in English 'fee').
[c; g]	are hard when followed by a, o, u, e.g., *la gare*; *comme*, but soft when followed by e, i, e.g., *ici*; *?ge*. To make a hard c or g soft, we use the following: (1) ç, e.g., *le garçon*; *nous commençons*; (2) e after the g, e.g., *nous mangeons*.

Note that when *oeuf* and *boeuf* are singular the f is pronounced, but in the plural the letter f is silent.
Similarly, when *un os* (a bone) is made plural the letter s is silent.

12.2 Homonyms

The following words often cause problems because they have the same (or almost the same) pronunciation.

1)	*il*	— he	2)	*elle*	— she
	Ils	— they		*elles*	— they
3)	*la*	— the	4)	*son*	— his, her
	là	— there		*sont*	— are
5)	*sa*	— his, her	6)	*ses*	— his, her
	ça	— that		*ces*	— these, those
7)	*de*	— of, from	8)	*sur*	— on
	deux	— two		*sûr*	— sure, safe
9)	*vingt*	— twenty	10)	*se*	— himself, etc.
	le vin	— wine		*ce*	— this, that
11)	*s'est*	— has	12)	*la fin*	— end
	c'est	— it is		*la faim*	— hunger
13)	*(tu) es*	— are	14)	*(tu) as*	— have
	(il) est	— is		*(il) a*	— has
				à	— to, at, in
15)	*on*	— one	16)	*si*	— if; so; yes
	ont	— have		*six*	— six
	en	— in, some etc.		*la scie*	— saw
17)	*la mer*	— sea	18)	*l'heure*	— hour, time
	la mère	— mother		*leur*	— to them; their
	le maire	— mayor		*leurs*	— their (pl.)
19)	*mes*	— my	20)	*quel*,etc.	— which? what? (+ *noun*)
	mais	— but			
	mai	— May		*qu'elle*	— that she (+ verb)
21)	*s'en (aller)*	— to go away	22)	*sept*	— seven
	cent	— hundred		*cette*	— this (f)
	le sang	— blood		*cet*	— this (m before vowel)
	sans	— without		*c'est*	— it is (as in *Il est un homme*)
23)	*(il) voi*	— sees	24)	*le pois*	— pea
	la voie	— way		*le poids*	— weight
	la voix	— voice		*la poix*	— pitch

25) *froid* — cold
    la fois — times
    la foi — faith
    le foie — liver
28) *toi* — you
    le toit — roof
30) *soi* — oneself
    (il) soit — may be
    la soie — silk

26) *droit* — right, straight
    le doigt — finger
27) *la tante* — aunt
    la tente — tent
29) *le père* — father
    le pair — peer
    la paire — pair

Faux-Amis

PART E

FAUX-AMIS

13 FAUX-AMIS

Literally meaning 'false friends', these are words which are deceptive, because, judged by their spelling or sound, they do not necessarily mean what one would expect them to mean. They make a fascinating list, e.g.:

Je reste à la maison — I'm staying at home. (To rest = *se reposer*.)
La cave est grande — the cellar is big. (cave = *la caverne*.)

accuser	— (also) to show
achever	— to complete
agréer	— to accept, to approve
aimer	— to like, to love
arriver	— (also) to happen, to occur
assister	— to attend
attendre	— to wait for
avertir	— to warn
balancer	— (also) to swing
blesser	— to wound, to injure
cacher	— to hide, to conceal
causer	— to chat
charger	— (also) to load
contrôler	— to inspect, to check
convenir	— to suit, to agree
défendre	— (also) to forbid, to prohibit
demander	— to ask
demeurer	— to live
déranger	— to disturb

dresser	—	to raise
heurter	—	to knock against, to bump into
hisser	—	to hoist
hurler	—	to howl
ignorer	—	to be ignorant of, not to know
labourer	—	to till, to plough
lier	—	to tie
nager	—	to swim
nommer	—	(also) to appoint
partir	—	to leave, to depart
passer (un examen)	—	to sit (an exam)
poser	—	to put down
prétendre	—	to claim
ramer	—	to row
rapporter	—	(usually) *to bring back*
regarder	—	(usually) to look at
remarquer	—	(usually) to notice
rentrer	—	to return (home)
répéter	—	(also) to rehearse
replier	—	to fold up
rester	—	to stay, to remain
retirer	—	to pull out, to extract
saluer	—	(also) to greet, to wave
se servir de	—	to use
sortir	—	to go out
supplier	—	to beg, to implore
supporter	—	(usually) to suffer, to put up with
surnommer	—	to nickname
taper	—	(also) to type
trainer	—	to drag
transpirer	—	(usually) to perspire
travailler	—	to work
trier	—	to sort out, to grade
l'adresse (f)	—	(also) skill
l'apologie (f)	—	defence, justification
l'argument (m)	—	discussion, summary, outline
l'assistance (f)	—	attendance, congregation
l'avertissement	—	warning, notice
la blouse	—	(usually) overall
le bond	—	leap, bound

Faux-Amis

le bras	—	arm
la brasse	—	fathom
la bride	—	bridle, reins
la bulle	—	(usually) bubble, blister
le cabinet	—	(usually) office, room, study, surgery, closet
la cane	—	duck
le car	—	(motor) coach
la casserole	—	saucepan
la cave	—	cellar
la chair	—	flesh
la chaire	—	pulpit
le champ	—	field
la chance	—	(usually) luck
le chandelier	—	candlestick
le chat	—	cat
le chip	—	potato-crisp
la cloche	—	bell
le coin	—	corner
le collège	—	school
le conducteur	—	driver
le contrôleur	—	(usually) inspector, examiner, ticket collector
la copie	—	(also) candidate's paper
la corne	—	horn
le corps	—	(living) body
la course	—	run, race, trip, outing
la cravate	—	tie
le curé	—	parish priest
la dent	—	tooth
la diète	—	(usually) starvation diet
le dogue	—	mastiff
l'èclair (m)	—	(usually) flash of lightning
l'essence (f)	—	(usually) petrol
l'étiquette (f)	—	(usually) label, ticket
l'évidence (f)	—	(usually) clearness
l'expérience (f)	—	(also) experiment
la fabrique	—	factory, manufacture
la farce	—	(also) practical joke, trick
la figure	—	face
la fin	—	end
la flèche	—	arrow, spire
la formation	—	(also) training

la foule	—	crowd
le four	—	oven, kiln, furnace
le front	—	(also) forehead
le gentilhomme	—	nobleman
le geste	—	gesture
la gorge	—	throat
l'habit (m)	—	coat, costume
le hasard	—	chance
l'herbe (f)	—	grass
l'hôte (f)	—	(female) guest
l'inconvénient (m)	—	disadvantage, drawback
l'injure (f)	—	insult
l'intelligence (f)	—	(usually) understanding, comprehension
la jalousie	—	(also) Venetian blind
la journée	—	(whole) day
le laboureur	—	ploughman
la lecture	—	reading
la librairie	—	bookshop
le magasin	—	(large) shop
la marmite	—	stewing-pot
la matinée	—	(whole) morning
le médecin	—	doctor
le membre	—	(also) limb
la messe	—	(Catholic) Mass
la mine	—	(also) appearance, look, expression, mien
la monnaie	—	(loose) change
la note	—	(also) bill, invoice, account, notice, mark
l'occasion (f)	—	opportunity, chance
l'opportunité (f)	—	opportuneness, timeliness, favourable occasion
le pain	—	bread
le pan	—	flap, shirt-tail
le pantalon	—	trousers
le parent	—	(also) relative
le pavé	—	cobblestone, paving stone
le pavement	—	ornamental tiling
la pension	—	(also) payment for board, boarding school (fees)
le pensionnaire	—	(also) boarder, resident, guest
la peste	—	(usually) plague
le pétrole	—	oil, petroleum
le photographe	—	photographer
la pièce	—	room, coin, play

Faux-Amis

la place	—	seat, town square
le plat	—	dish
le plateau	—	(also) tray
le plongeur	—	(also) washer-up
la promenade	—	walk
la queue	—	(also) tail
la rate	—	spleen
le regard	—	look, gaze
les reins (m)	—	kidneys
la répétition	—	(also) rehearsal
les restes (m)	—	remains
la ride	—	wrinkle
le roman	—	novel
le sable	—	sand
la serviette	—	(also) towel, briefcase
le siège	—	(also) seat
le singe	—	monkey
le slip	—	(under)pants
le smoking	—	dinner-jacket
le stage	—	course, probationary period
le sud	—	south
le talon	—	(usually) heel
le timbre	—	postage stamp
la toilette	—	wash(ing), dressing, getting ready; washstand
le tour	—	(also) turn, trick
la tour	—	tower, rook (chess)
le travail	—	work
les vacances (f)	—	holidays, vacation
le vague	—	vagueness
la vague	—	wave
la vase	—	(river) mud
le verger	—	orchard
le vers	—	line (of poetry)
la veste	—	jacket
le veston	—	jacket
les waters (m)	—	toilet
actuel	—	of the present day, current
actuellement	—	at present, at the moment
ancien	—	(also) former, ex-
blanc	—	white

blessé	—	wounded, injured
brave	—	(also) good, honest, worthy
car	—	for
en train de	—	engaged in, in the process of
fatal	—	(also) fateful, inevitable
génial	—	brilliant, inspired
gentil	—	kind, nice
inhabité	—	uninhabited
joli	—	pretty
laid	—	ugly
large	—	wide
merci	—	thank you
mince	—	thin
or	—	now, well
pour	—	for, in order to
sensible	—	sensitive
surnommé	—	nicknamed
sympathique	—	(usually) likeable, pleasant
unique	—	only, single, sole
usé	—	worn out, shabby
vilain	—	mean, ugly, wicked

PART F
14 ESSAY WRITING

(1)   DO write *simple* French *correctly*.

(2)   DO try to think in French as much as possible.

(3)   DO think of phrases, idioms, etc., which you have seen previously, and incorporate them *if relevant* into your essay.

(4)   DO pay careful attention to *spelling, agreements, accents, number and gender*.

(5)   DO use all the information available in a guided essay, i.e. listen carefully to readings, and make use of any questions beneath pictures from the point of grammar, spelling etc.

(1)   DO NOT think of a *sophisticated* English sentence, and attempt to translate word for word.

(2)   DO NOT translate a phrase one word at a time, but try to think what the French would say.

(3)   DO NOT write more than is necessary, if this is at the expense of accuracy.

PART G
15 JUST FOR FUN

15.1 Tongue Twisters

(1) *Didon dîna, dit-on, de dix dodus dos de dix dodus dindons.*
(2) *Un chasseur sachant chasser doit savoir chasser sans son chien.*
(3) *C'est combien ces six cent six saucissons-ci? C'est six cent six sous ces six cent six saucissons-ci.*
(4) *Si six scies scient six cyprès, six cent six scies scient six cent six cyprès.*
(5) *Le vers est: le ver vert va vers le verre vert et vertical.*
(6) *Les chaussettes de l'archiduchesse sont-elles sèches? Archisèches.*

15.2 Conundrum

Q. *Pourquoi ne faut-il pas trop nourrir un nain?*
A. *Parce qu'on risque d'en faire un ingrat (nain gras).*

15.3 Quick Quiz

(1) Find a six letter French word containing all five vowels.
(2) Find two French words where the letter 'Q' is not followed by the letter 'u'.
(3) Find two basic French words which can be pronounced in three different ways.
(4) Find a French word which contains a 'c' pronounced as a 'g'.
(5) Find a French word which changes completely in the plural.
(6) Find a French word beginning with a vowel, which is preceded by le and not l'.
(7) Find a French word containing the letter 'e' three times in a row.
(8) Find three French words which are masculine in the singular but are, or can be, feminine in the plural.

Faux-Amis

15.4 Proverbs

Pair up the following proverbs:

(1) A bon chat, bon rat.
(2) A cheval donné on ne regarde pas les dents.
(3) Après la pluie, le beau temps.
(4) C'est en forgeant qu'on deviant forgeron.
(5) Il faut casser le noyau pour avoir l'amande.
(6) Impossible n'est pas français.
(7) Le mieux est l'ennemi du bien.
(8) Mieux vaut tard que jamais.
(9) On ne peut pas avoir le beurre et l'argent du beurre.
(10) On ne peut pas être à la fois au four et au moulin.
(11) Quand on veut, on peut.
(12) Qui ne risque rien n'a rien.
(13) Qui se sent morveux, qu'il se mouche.
(14) Tous les goûts sont dans la nature.
(15) Tout est bien qui finit bien.
(16) Un sou est un sou.

(A) Practice makes perfect.
(B) Every penny counts.
(C) You can't have your cake and eat it.
(D) Better late than never.
(E) It takes all kinds to make a world.
(F) If the cap fits, wear it.
(G) All's well that ends well.
(H) Don't look the gifthorse in the mouth.
(I) Every cloud has a silver lining.
(J) No pain, no gain.
(K) Leave well alone.
(L) Nothing ventured, nothing gained.
(M) Tit for Tat.
(N) Where there's a will, there's a way.
(O) There's no such word as 'can't'.
(P) You can't be in two places at once.

Answers to Quiz and Proverbs at back of book (see pages 65-66)

PART H
16 SUPPLEMENT

The *passé simple* is included in this book for recognition purposes, since A-level students may well have access to a more literary type of French, where they would meet this tense.

The Past Anterior, and the Present Tense of the Subjunctive Mood, are likewise included for completeness, in order to assist students who take the subject beyond the confines of Common Entrance and GCSE.

16.1 Past Historic Tense — *le passé simple*

(1) The past historic is sometimes called the past <u>definite</u>, <u>preterite</u> or <u>aorist</u>.
(2) It is a simple past tense, i.e. it has only one part, whereas the Perfect Tense has two.
(3) Its use is confined to written French, i.e. literature of all kinds.
(4) It is equivalent to the English 'I went' (*J'allai*), but not I have gone which must be translated as *je suis allé*.

Formation

Regular verbs + *aller*:

<u>A group</u>	<u>I group</u>	
Donner (er)	Finir (ir)	Vendre (re)
Je donnai — I gave	*Je finis* - I finished	*Je vendis* — I sold
Tu donnas	*Tu finis*	*Tu vendis*
Il donna	*Il finit*	*Il vendit*
Nous donnâmes	*Nous finîmes*	*Nous vendîmes*
Vous donnâtes	*Vous finîtes*	Vous vendîtes
Ils donnèrent	*Ils finirent*	*Ils vendirent*

NB. Care must be taken with regular *-ir* verbs in the singular because *je finis* = I am finishing (present), and I finished (past).

Verbs ending in *-oir* and *-oire* (except *voir*, *s'asseoir*):

U group

Vouloir

Je voulus — I wanted
Tu voulus
Il voulut
Nous voulûmes
Vous voulûtes
Ils voulurent

Irregular verbs:

The *passé simple* can often be formed from the <u>past participle</u> of the verb in question, e.g.:

avoir	— *j'ai eu*	—	*j'eus*
dire	— *j'ai dit*	—	*je dis*
prendre	— *j'ai pris*	—	*je pris*

Common exceptions:

être (to be)	— *je fus*
faire (to make, to do)	— *je fis*
écrire (to write)	— *j'écrivis*
couvrir (to cover)	— *je couvris*
ouvrir (to open)	— *j'ouvris*
souffrir (to suffer)	— *je souffris*
offrir (to offer)	— *j'offris*
naître (to be born)	— *je naquis*
vaincre (to conquer)	— *je vainquis*
voir (to see)	— *je vis*
mourir (to die)	— *je mourus*
venir (to come)	— *je vins*
tenir (to hold)	— *je tins*

16.2 Past Anterior Tense — *le passé antérieur*

(1) The past anterior is a *compound* tense.
(2) Its use is confined basically to written French.
(3) It is equivalent to the English pluperfect.
(4) It is used in subordinate clauses after certain temporal conjunctions when one action is immediately followed by a second in the past tense.
(5) The main clause must be in the past historic.

Conjunctions

quand \
lorsque } — when

aussitôt que \
dès que } — as soon as

aprés que — after

NB. It is also used after the adverb à *peine ... que* — scarcely ... than, which requires inversion of subject and verb.

Aide-mémoire — an Equation:

Past Historic of *avoir or être* + *past* participle = Past Anterior, e.g.:

J'eus vendu — I had sold.
Il eut dit — he had said.
Nous fûmes arrivés — we had arrived.

Use of the past anterior:

Quand ils <u>eurent préparé</u> leur pique-nique, ils <u>partirent</u> — When they *had prepared* their picnic, they *set* off.

Aussitôt qu'elle <u>fut arrivée</u>, elle <u>s'assit</u> — As soon as she <u>had arrived</u>, she <u>sat down</u>.

16.3 Subjunctive Mood — *le subjonctif*

(1) The subjunctive mood is used comparatively rarely in French to state suppositions rather than facts (indicative mood).

(2) It is equivalent to the English if <u>I were you</u>; <u>God bless you</u>; <u>if this be true</u>, etc.

(3) It is used after:

   (a) Verbs which express desire,
   (b) Verbs which express emotion,
   (c) Verbs which express uncertainty,
   (d) A superlative expression,
   (e) An impersonal verb or expression,
   (f) Certain adverbial conjunctions.

(4) In general there is a toning down of certainty or likelihood.

(5) The subjunctive has four tenses in French: the present, imperfect, perfect and pluperfect. The present tense is certainly the most important of the four tenses.

16.4 Formation of the Present Subjunctive — *le présent du subjonctif*

General Rule:

Remove the *-nt* from the 3rd person plural Present Tense, to get the 1st person singular of the Present Subjunctive, e.g.:

attendre	—	*ils attend<u>ent</u>*	—	*j'attend<u>e</u>*
boire	—	*ils boi<u>vent</u>*	—	*je boiv<u>e</u>*

Remove the *-ons* from the lst person plural Present Tense to get the stem of the lst and 2nd plural Present Subjunctive, e.g.:

boire	—	*nous buv<u>ons</u>*	—	*nous buv<u>ions</u>*
jeter	—	*nous jet<u>ons</u>*	—	*nous jet<u>ions</u>*

Endings:

-e, -es, -e, -ions, -iez, -ent, e.g.:

Finir	*Prendre*	*Voir*
Je finisse	*Je prenne*	*Je voie*
Tu finisses	*Tu prennes*	*Tu voies*
Il finisse	*Il prenne*	*Il voie*
Nous finissions	*Nous prenions*	*Nous voyions*
Vous finissiez	*Vous preniez*	*Vous voyiez*
Ils finissent	*Ils prennent*	*Ils voient*

Important exceptions:

Être	*Avoir*	*Aller*
Je sois	*J'aie*	*J'aille*
Tu sois	*Tu aies*	*Tu ailles*
Il soit	*Il ait*	*Il aille*
Nous soyons	*Nous ayons*	*Nous allions*
Vous soyez	*Vous ayez*	*Vous alliez*
Ils soient	*Ils aient*	*Ils aillent*

Faire	*Pouvoir*	*Vouloir*
Je fasse	*Je puisse*	*Je veuille*
Tu fasses	*Tu puisses*	*Tu veuilles*
Il fasse	*Il puisse*	*Il veuille*
Nous fassions	*Nous puissions*	*Nous voulions*
Vous fassiez	*Vous puissiez*	*Vous vouliez*
Ils fassent	*Ils puissant*	*Ils veuillent*

Note Also:

Savoir	—	*Je sache, etc.*
Pleuvoir	—	*Il pleuve*
Falloir	—	*Il faille*

Supplement: Subjunctive Mood

16.5 Uses of the Subjunctive

It is used after the following:

vouloir que ...	— to wish that	} desire
regretter que	— to regret that	
c'est dommage que	— it is a pity that	} emotion
être content que	— to be pleased that	
avoir peur que ... ne (+ subj. verb)	— to be afraid that	
je ne crois pas que	— I don't think that	} uncertainty
croyez-vous que ... ?	— do you think that ... ?	
il est possible que	— it is possible that	} impersonal expressions
il est impossible que	— it is impossible that	
il faut que ...	— you must	
quoique	— although	} adverbial conjunctions
bien que	—	
pour que	— in order that	
afin que	— so that	
sans que	— without	
avant que	— before	
jusqu' à ce que	— until	
(attendre que	— to wait until*)*	
à moins que ... ne (+ subj. verb)	— unless	

17 Answers to Quiz

(1) *oiseau*
(2) *cinq; coq*
(3) *six; dix*
(4) *second(e); secondaire*
(5) *oeil* (pl. *les yeux*)
(6) *onze* (e.g. *le onze mai*)
(7) *créée*
(8) *amour; délice; orgue*

Answers to Proverbs:

(1) M	(2) H
(3) I	(4) A
(5) J	(6) O
(7) K	(8) D
(9) C	(10) P
(11) N	(12) L
(13) F	(14) E
(15) G	(16) B

18 GLOSSARY

An explanation of some of the grammatical terms used in this book:

Direct object:
A noun or pronoun which directly receives the action of the verb,
e.g.: *je vois l'homme* — I see the man.
 je le vois — I see him.

Indirect object:
A noun or pronoun which indirectly receives the action of the verb,
e.g.: *je lui donne le livre* — I give the book to him;
 I give him the book.

Reflexive object:
A pronoun which refers back to the subject of the sentence,
e.g.: *je me lave* — I wash (myself).

Disjunctive pronoun:
A strong pronoun, i.e. one which is not attached to a verb in such a way as to have a direct grammatical relationship with it,
e.g.: *Qui a ouvert la porte? Lui? Non, elle* — Who opened the door? Did he? No, she did. (Contrast conjunctive or weak pronouns.)

Present Participle:
The form of the verb which ends in *-ant* in French and -ing in English,
e.g.: *donnant* — giving.

Imperative Mood:
The command form of the verb (from Latin *impero* — I command),
e.g.: *lève-toi!*; *levez-vous!* — stand up!

Subjunctive Mood:
A form of the verb used when the content of the clause is being doubted, supposed, wished or thought, rather than asserted,
e.g.: *Je souhaite que tu viennes pendant les vacances de Pâques* —
 I wish you would come during the Easter holidays.